Old Inveraray & Upper Loch Fy
by John MacLeay

Inveraray, Main Street.   C.S.429

Main Street is here seen some 20 years, and a World War, later than the picture opposite. This angle, a few doors down from the George Hotel, shows the railed-off Celtic cross, once thought to have come from Iona, a theory now discounted. For centuries it was the market cross and 'many a proclamation and many a hanging and beheading it has seen', the historian George Eyre-Todd reflected: for him it was the burgh's 'only antiquity of note'. With the building of the new town, 'it lay useless and neglected' before being 'restored to its rightful place of honour as central ornament of the town' in the latter half of the nineteenth century. On the left-hand side of the street we see what appears to be a coat of arms above one shop (neither the Duke of Argyll's nor the burgh's) but no such device appears here today. In front there seem to be peats being delivered from a handcart, but motor vehicles are beginning to make their presence known, although we're still a long way from the day when the burgh would be described as 'just one more snarled knot of holiday traffic', and the 'hump-backed bridges are cursed by drivers'.

Text © John MacLeay, 2007
First published in the United Kingdom, 2007,
by Stenlake Publishing Ltd.
www.stenlake.co.uk
ISBN 9781840333923

Acknowledgments

My thanks are due to Jeannie and Terry for their patience through seemingly endless computer snags. I am also indebted to many kindly Loch Fyneside folk, for their help and company while I was engaged on my researches, chiefly Donald Clark, Reg Witt, Ewan Jenkins and Don Sturrock. I received valuable help from John Hamilton and Jeff Dodds of Enstone Thistle at the Furnace quarry, from some friendly gents at the tea-room facing Crarae Quarry, from staff in the George Hotel and the Argyll Arms, Inveraray, and in the Clachan, Strachur. I gratefully acknowledge a debt to the works of 'local boy' Neil Munro, especially observations by his best-known creation, Para Handy who, after all, 'wass born along this Lochside'. The Birlinn edition of these tales contains pages of useful notes on the 20-year period in which they are set.

Further Reading

The books listed below were used by the author during his research. None of them is available from Stenlake Publishing. Those interested in finding out more are advised to contact their local bookshop or library service.

J. J. Bell, *Scotland's Rainbow West*, G. G. Harrap, London (1933).

George Blake, *The Firth of Clyde*, Collins, London (1952).

Marion Campbell, *Argyll: The Enduring Heartland*,
    Turnstone Books, London (1977).

Ian G. Lindsay and Mary Cosh, *Inveraray and the Dukes of Argyll*,
    Edinburgh University Press.

W. H. Murray, *The Companion Guide to the West Highlands of Scotland*,
    William Collins and Sons, London (1977).

Nigel Tranter, *The Queen's Scotland: Argyll And Bute*,
    Hodder and Stoughton, London (1977).

W. Weyndling, *Ferry Tales of Argyll and the Isles*, Allan Sutton, Stroud (1996).

Author's note: Gaelic and Anglicised Gaelic names or terms, italicised in the text, are not standardised in spelling, but spelled as in the various sources consulted.

The watchtower on the craggy, conical 800-foot hill of Duniquaich above Inveraray Castle is a folly dating from 1749, when pacification after the failed Rising had finally made 'watch and ward' on the passes no longer necessary, but there had been towers here before. 'Dun' generally indicates a fortified height and from Pictish times this had served as a look-out post with a beacon ready to be kindled in times of emergency. The Gaelic name means 'hill of the cup', perhaps in allusion to its shape or in connection with a healing or holy well or possibly just a welcome spring, although the nearest water is some way below the summit.

INTRODUCTION

Along our longest sea loch, seemingly every other food outlet offers 'Fyne' fish or other fare, while down the centuries various attractions have guaranteed a 'Fyne' time. The name has been spelled in various ways, from 'Finne' to the 'Finny loch', the latter recalling the old local boast that the loch is three parts fish to one of water. That is no longer the case, with many of the loch's harbours now devoid of fishing craft – a contrast with the famed era when 'it wass the herrins of Loch Fyne had the reputation', in an age of 'high jeenks and big hauls; you werena very smart if you werena into both'. Once traders had called at Inveraray's French Foreland 'to swap casks of claret wine for the finest herrings in the whole world' and later still as many as 600 vessels were engaged in gathering this 'silver harvest of the sea'.

There was always more, though, to this deep-probing 40-mile inlet than barrels and boxes of kippers or 'Glasgow magistrates'. Taking its name from a Gaelic word, Fyne means clear, bright, even shining, all words that, when applied to weather, *do* mean fine. Between Skate (an islet) and Otter (a constricting, mile-long sandbank), the loch is a north-easterly extension of the Kilbrannan Sound that separates Arran and Kintyre.

Upper Loch Fyne has scale, charm to spare, and a light that works its own *glamourie* even on smirry, overcast days when the mist itself can have a shimmering quality that dazzles the eyes, the bobbing weed on the tide's edge is turned into gold as though by some warlock's spell and the pebbles underfoot have the sheen of semi-precious stones. That light may throw sinister shadows, yet minutes later bring about a kindlier mood. Duniquaich, as brawny as many a greater height, rears clear of the tree line like some giant throwing off his pelt, while higher, bald crests can seem as benign as monkish tonsures. In such a light the very place-names have their own enchantment: Kilcatrine giving off a quiet blessing, while there's a dour growl to Cairndhu when we know that it means the black cairn, a note of prickly arrogance to both Ardkinglas and Dunderave, whereas Dalchenna is as soft as anything crooned in a cradle-song. Here on the upper loch are all the charm and contrast of what Marion Campbell of Kilberry described as hill-country into which the sea has bitten deep.

Although hugely plundered in the past, the 'chief plume of Loch Fyne is the natural wood extending down to the coastal strip on both sides … wood, water and mountain combine to enrich much of Argyll'. This whole region splendidly combines the wild with the civilised, and civilised the folk living in Argyll are, be they cheery, chatty bus-drivers or folk in tiny, truly quaint, post offices where talk is as valued as trade and there's a courteous curiosity towards anyone 'after information' about their locality. In all, a delightfully varied quarter, and a setting worthy of the finest jewel, and that it has in the form of *Bhail Inbhiraora*.

That – with a clue as to the correct pronunciation is how Inveraray appears in the title of a pipe tune about 'a wedding in the town of Inveraray', a tune you'll know if you've sung 'The Campbells are Coming'. And come they did, from their lands in the long shadows of Cruachan Ben, a hill out of sight on the River Aray's banks, but vividly remembered, probably visualised, when their battle cry was yelled. Here on Fyneside and beyond were territories for the taking, much of them forfeited Clan Donald lands. Deep waters just offshore provided an out-gate to the wider world, making Inveraray a port (with its own 'foreign quarter' down on the French Foreland) at a time when Glasgow's merchants still had to see their cargoes unloaded 20 miles downriver. The Campbells' expansion and rise were rapid, resentment or ill will taken as mere recognition of their success and influence, and they became as much dynasty as clan; at times something akin to a rival state or royalty. The town grew, its buildings springing up to create 'a dirty ill-built village', but still the heart of what became the original 'Campbell's Kingdom'. Only two years after it had been sacked and burned in his name (in December 1644) did Charles I accord it royal burgh status, but it remained the seat of power, a noted lady of the clan likening it to a spider's web twitching to every tug, but emphasising that the pull did not always come from the centre, lesser Campbell chiefs being jealous of their own autonomy and authority.

The overall head, Campbell of Argyll, whether as earl, marquis or latterly duke, was always *MacCalein Mhor*, by whichever spelling, Son of Great Colin, and if the ill-disposed grumbled about 'King Campbell', he might not have been wholly displeased. Long centuries of warring finally at an end in 1746, the 3rd Duke resumed the interrupted plans for rebuilding both castle and township, 'that most depressing of fish-smelling of Highland towns' being not only rebuilt but relocated to the bracing Gallows Foreland, where the winds possibly cleared it of the more oppressive memories of 'old unhappy far-off things', if not of 'battles long-ago'. The castle has its critics, but the town is a triumph, truly 'designed to delight the eye from every angle of approach, both by land and water'. A perfect place to finish any day; an ideal spot in which to spend an entire day. And so genuinely friendly, that even ardent Jacobites can be enchanted by it.

While there's still every chance of seeing an otter at Otter Ferry, you'll look in vain for a ferry. According to the author of *Ferry Tales*, while cattle were no longer transported, the service was still operational until the Second World War, continuing in a reduced capacity after the war. The 'Oitir' (Gaelic) is a mile-long gravel spit jutting from the Cowal shore, constricting the navigable fairway to three-quarters of a mile at low water, making this a logical – possibly the earliest – crossing spot. Before there was any ferry, cattle could be 'swum' across the loch, still a practice in recent decades between the Inner Isles and the mainland. This cattle trade, as much as passengers, brought about improvements to piers and quays and the increased size of vessels. Here, close to Port Ann, between Lochs Gair and Gilp on the western side of the 'narrows' separating Outer and Upper Loch Fyne, the narrator of Neil Munro's *John Splendid* noted how 'the bulk of the boats are down at Otter, damming the fish in the narrow gut and keeping them from searching up to our own good townsmen' in Inveraray, an instance of turning a navigation hazard or obstruction to advantage. The men of Lochlann (Vikings) had also utilised it as a beaching post for their dragon ships on one of their swoops on Cowal.

Otter Ferry.

C.S. 309.

Across the loch from the picture on the page opposite, on the eastern side, lies the small village of Otter Ferry itself. The bare trees give a bleak look to these buildings, the nearer of which was the post office – the signboard can just be seen over the door. The postmaster, postmistress or someone in the household seems to have kept livestock, if only for milk and eggs, possibly vended on the premises. The road branching off offers a route through to Kames or the 'High Road to Glendaruel', to use the title of a fine pipe tune, over the Ballochandrain (Pass of the Briars) giving an outlook to the Inner Isles. It is hard to associate this with the days of the thriving cattle trade. This locality was also famed for its oysters, happily still obtainable in some hotels. The sturdy quay now has a neglected look, but yachting folk still retain a liking for this delightfully quiet area with its views across the widening loch to Knapdale.

A drinking fountain by Auchgoyle Bay tells us only that Sir Thomas Lloyd lived from 1835 to 1905, but his fine Scots Baronial mansion, Minard Castle, enjoys more seclusion than this shot suggests, almost surrounded by picturesque woodlands that screen it from the main road, while allowing access to quiet stretches of shoreline with uninterrupted views towards Strathlachlan and the 'Kerry coast'. Since its first owner's day it has alternated as private residence and hotel. A cargo vessel built in 1882, hauling freight, livestock and passengers on the Glasgow–Inveraray run for nearly 50 years may have taken its name, *Minard Castle*, from an earlier fortification in this area.

Minard

View from the Sea, Minard.

The stark lines of what were once dismissed as 'bungaloid growths' may seem a bit out of keeping at Minard, but the surrounding greenery and their own gardens have long softened any rawness, allowing them to blend in with the landscape and enjoy a stunning outlook beyond Auchgoyle Bay and Ferry Point towards some striking islets (a rarity on Loch Fyne). The scene is little changed from how it was in the mid-1930s, although this being the main road leading through Knapdale and Kintyre to Campbeltown, traffic lights are now a necessary feature.

Heavy traffic has called for road-widening along much of this route towards Furnace at Crarae, but it remains a pleasure to walk, most of the building being on the landward side of the road, with an unobstructed outlook across the loch and along the coast. These cottages (looking southwards, back towards Minard) back onto the shore, still readily identifiable, though re-roofed. A hundred yards from the massive Crarae Quarry, these may have been built for the workers. The quarry, where now the sounds of blasting are replaced by the mewing of buzzards, was the scene of a disaster involving not workers, but trippers. In June 1886 it was advertised that an unusually large amount of explosive was to be used in blasting operations, and a steamer-trip on the original *Lord of the Isles* was laid on for those keen to witness this. After the blast some onlookers, seeking a closer look, were overcome by dust and fumes, and seven of them died. There was an old tale that this was taken as a sign of divine disapproval visited on those who had violated the Sabbath, but a Greenock newspaper report confirms that the tragedy actually took place on a Saturday.

Some writers have found granite, gardens and greenery an incongruous teaming, but a generous rainfall and the benign Gulf Stream's influence make much of Argyll favourable to a huge variety of exotic and spectacular flora and trees. Crarae Lodge is seen here in 1910. In the following decade Sir George Campbell of Succoth extended and developed the gardens, utilising the glen behind his home, which has been likened to a Himalayan gorge or even a rainforest. The house itself was damaged in the 1970s but is now restored and the gardens are a year-round attraction. Although much less extensive than Benmore Gardens or the gardens at Ardkinglas, Crarae is probably the most visited.

Sandhole, Furnace, is seen here in the early twentieth century. Any earlier Gaelic name remains elusive, but Sandhole itself is suggestive of sand-extraction, a conjecture supported by the figure with the wheelbarrow. While sand had uses in foundries, for building and on the land, sea sand is not always suited to industrial purposes, nor are sand deposits all that common along the silt, shingle, mud and rock beaches of the 'Clyde lochs'. It does occur, though, in a few small bays where streams, like that which the man has crossed, meet the sea. While no one knows of its ever being put to any commercial or industrial use, this is a spot where it was at least obtainable.

A plentiful supply of timber led to the establishment in Argyll of gunpowder manufacture (dependent on charcoal), while much other wood was hauled away to feed 'bloomeries' (industrial furnaces). The discovery of ironstone locally made it logical to site such a smelter here at the mouth of Glen Leacann. While there were already small forges and foundries throughout the Highlands, there was probably no Gaelic word for furnace, hence the name Furnace replaced the old Inverlechan. The Goatfield furnace (seen here around 1905), a surprisingly unobtrusive structure for its size, was installed in 1755 by a Cumbrian firm for some Lancashire iron masters, and had ceased to operate by 1813. The view was held, not just locally, that the furnace was erected simply to destroy all the local timber that had for so long sheltered fugitives, 'broken men' and those 'put to the horn' (formally outlawed), but it was too valuable for shipbuilding and other industrial purposes simply to squander. The gunpowder works blew up 70 years later, in 1883 – mercifully on a day when the prevailing wind had changed direction. By this time explosions had become a feature of life, thanks to the booming (in every sense) quarrying industry. The main difference in this scene in Furnace today is the much-widened road, required for the heavy vehicles that used to call at the nearby quarry, possibly where the horse and cart are headed.

At Furnace and Dunlechan, seen here around 1920, very near the old furnace, the landscape is almost the same today, and some of the buildings are still there too. The barn-like structure to the left was until recently the 'coal ree' or depot. There is some modern housing in the area to the rear. The foreground area is now largely taken up by a fish-farming venture, somewhat restricting the use of clothes-lines. The trees screen a complex of quarries, one being known as 'California', apparently due to its being worked by men who had tried their luck in the '49 gold rush, presumably with limited success.

Furnace

The Quarry, Furnace.

Today the steam crane and adjoining buildings of a century ago would be preserved as industrial archaeology, but the quarry at Furnace remains a going concern (Enstone Thistle), the hoppers, crushing machinery and other modern plant and installations making it highly visible all along the coast road from Minard – though curiously, in Furnace itself, it seems discreetly tucked away. The scene, however, remains recognisable, the basin or wharf neglected but reasonably intact, allowing us a glimpse into the logistics of the local economy. Timber was plentiful here and easily shipped out, as were quarry stone, iron ore ingots from the nearby smelter and the locally manufactured gunpowder. Among many other uses, stone from here went to pave Glasgow's streets. Close by, near Auchindrain, by the Leacann Water, the last wolf in Mid-Argyll was slain some time in the first half of the eighteenth century. The weapon of choice was a spindle but the valiant lady did not long outlive her lupine victim. This story occurs in several Highland localities, always involving a woman and a household implement, always around the same period. Myth, allegory or outright prophecy of the womenfolk gaining the upper hand?

Dalchenna House (pronounced Dalhenna), seen here in the early years of the twentieth century, was demolished in the early 1990s, to much local annoyance and distress. In 1755 Inveraray wig-maker Peter Campbell had a career change, becoming 'riding officer' or surveyor of customs and was granted land at Dalchenna Point, some two miles south of the burgh, for the erection of two small houses. One later became a 'spinning house', whether as a place of instruction or manufacture is not clear, but this building supplanted both. A dower house of the Argyll family, it became the home of the widowed Princess Louise, daughter of Queen Victoria, who had married into the ducal household. That union supposedly prompted the remark: 'Aye, it's the proud woman the Queen must be this day for her daughter to be getting the son of Mic Cailean Mhor for her husband.' During the Second World War the house served as accommodation for locally based Wrens, operating later as a hotel.

The ramshackle charm lent to this tiny building by the wooden structures give it the appeal of an Arthur Rackham painting, but while its size and setting are those of a lodge, no one recalls its being occupied in that capacity. A locally voiced, if tongue-in-cheek, theory suggests that it was a play-house for the Duke's children – improbable, but the dimensions *are* tiny, illustrated by the poultry in the low doorway. Facing the shore midway between Dalchenna Point and Newtown, it goes by the name East Cromalt today. In Neil Munro's *John Splendid* there are references to coming at Inveraray from 'the Cromalt end' (that is, from the south). *Cromalt* indicates the crooked or winding stream which joins the loch close by and from which pearls were occasionally obtained, to be utilised in locally made jewellery. In later years Munro gave this name to his Helensburgh home.

Shown here as it was a century ago, Newtown is the prosaically named southern extension of Inveraray, a quarter-mile length of buildings, several of them one-time religious meeting-houses, which effectively conceal more recent housing, thus maintaining a harmonious continuity to the town. Today's traffic no longer favours the leisurely perambulations of cattle, but it remains a pleasing spot, hard by the loch's edge, allowing a view of the burgh from a less familiar angle. Beyond the trees lies the former MacBride's Hotel (now the Inveraray), wartime HQ for Combined Operations in a period when the upper loch saw practice for amphibious landings, in a terrain more rugged by far than many invasion zones in Europe or Africa. It is easy to imagine this length of coastline being a pleasant memory for many who fell on distant beaches. Some of the Polish troops who went through the gruelling training here remained or returned, working within the forestry and building trades locally.

Taken about a century ago, just offshore from Newtown, this view of Inveraray towards 'the ramparts' behind the old prison on the one-time Gallows Foreland, often under siege from the waves, emphasises what Marion Campbell dubbed its 'frontier town' aspect. The Second World War years led to the loss of the distinctive spire on the church for, already a bit shaky, it was further threatened by the constant movement of military vehicles, wheeled and tracked. In 1941 it was dismantled and apparently put to ignominious use as road rubble. Without it the church today looks undeniably squat. The tenement to the left, in front of the church, now houses the post office. Back on the 'foreland' the row of one-time wash-houses is now converted to dwellings and in the same vicinity is author Neil Munro's birthplace. The superb backdrop is supplied by Duniquaich, as much guardian spirit as mere hill. Only some 800 feet high, it has the contours and character of loftier heights, its crags rearing aggressively up clear of the tree line, though J. J. Bell saw it as essentially benevolent, casting a 'benediction' over town and castle, a mood superbly caught in this picture. It is worth noting too how well those tenements, or 'lands', much reviled elsewhere, blend into the 'townscape'.

Inveraray's Palladian-style parish church was long a two-in-one affair, with one side for Gaelic services while those in the other half were conducted in English for the ducal household and staff, an arrangement that occasioned caustic observations about a wall dividing God's worshippers. Today the former Gaelic half serves as the church hall and even minus the spire it makes a splendid contrasting focal point to the spacious but homely street. Its siting, though, greatly displeased one inebriated soul unlucky enough to collide with its wall. 'Yon's a helluva place tae put a kirk,' he sourly commented. The demeanour of 'Postie' suggests that photography in the early 1920s was not the commonplace activity so familiar today. Inveraray remains a county town (though with the population – 500 – of a village) and ducal capital, still with that air of a frontier. For all the incongruities it remains firmly Scottish, Lowland in its domestic architecture but wholly Highland in setting, spirit and atmosphere.

The George Hotel, at the top of Main Street, has been in the Clark family for six generations, and the name can be seen above the door in this photograph, the most recent in this book. The cars, the lines of the touring coach (Trent, a Midlands company), the street markings, and a 'modern' lamp-post all indicate the 1950s, when motorists with the right badges were saluted by motorcyclist road-scouts, not entirely the drab, austere era that many seem to recall. The present proprietor of the George, Donald Clark, recalls this photograph being taken back in his schooldays. The sign on the lamp standard indicates that the post office has changed premises, while another on the hotel announces the friendly public bar (at the far right), with its flagstone floor and a welcoming fire in season. Here, the 'peat fire flame' is no mere song title and is a grand spot to meet the locals and the genial Donald himself. This old, genuinely atmospheric coaching inn is diagonally opposite the front of the parish church.

A century has effected few changes on Front Street, although today the only 'paddler' seen in these waters is the ageing *Waverley*. Paddles are generally associated with much larger craft but in the 1860s the Inveraray Ferry and Coach Company (with which the then duke was involved) commissioned a ferry called the *Fairy*. A mere 60 feet long, with a 13-foot beam, this vessel plied to Strachur to link up with the horse-drawn coaches. The steamer shown here may be its replacement, bearing the same name, coming into service in the early 1900s, captained on occasion by a local man named McKellar. She was wrecked in a gale in 1912. The arches, such a conspicuous feature of the town, at this period still fronted an ancient avenue of beech trees, felled during the Second World War. Now they screen what is essentially a parking area, although some replanting has taken place. The tall building to the right is the Argyll Arms, where Dr Johnson, eager to discover what 'makes a Scotsman truly happy', sampled his first – and only – dram. A less contented visitor, Burns, came up with some unusually rancorous lines about 'Heilan pride and Heilan scab and hunger', uncomplimentary to both the populace and 'the king of kings, His Grace'. Here, until 1962, the judges lodged, the well-stocked cellar being seen as a tribute to their 'judgement'. The solitary arch adjoining spans the road leading towards Loch Awe and Oban, while the small lodge on the far right is by the entrance to the castle grounds.

This stretch of the front is not yet railed off in this view from the 1920s, but there has been some reinforcing of the stonework by the water's edge. The smoke from the steam lighter's funnel eloquently explains the term 'puffer', a craft long regarded with affection by many even before Neil Munro's Para Handy stories, as witnessed by the *Maggie*, filmed long before the *Vital Spark* voyaged across our TV screens. From the 1880s this was the unglamorous work-horse of 'all the seas that lie between Bowling and Stornoway', transporting not only coal but 'whunstone, and oak bark and timber and trash like that'. Though largely linked with the Clyde, West Coast and the Isles, these craft were constructed to fit into the 70-foot locks of the Forth and Clyde Canal, many as far inland on that waterway as Kirkintilloch. They fetched building materials for the expanding resorts, occasionally carried the mail, undertook 'flittings' and carried gravel, ore and scrap metal. It was probably hard, dirty, demanding work, but compared with the formalities and protocol of larger vessels, their crews appeared to enjoy an enviable air of freedom and independence. Happily, today at this very berth you can board a lovable 'tarry old hooker' like that shown.

'If you haven't been at your favourite coast resort except at the time of summer holidays,' explained son of the burgh Neil Munro, you don't know much about it. In those dozing, dreamy days', it looked, sounded and more importantly, smelled differently, 'the one sound in the morning … the sizzle of frying herring … peace broods on the place like a benediction and (by the odour) someone is having a sheep's head singed at the smithy.' That was a popular mid-week dish back at the turn of the twentieth century, which this postcard perhaps pre-dates. This truly tranquil scene has the hushed mood of early morning in just such a season when, as Marion Campbell of Kilberry recalls, 'a metal bar dropped in a garage clangs like a sword'.

LORD OF THE ISLES AT INVERARAY

Compared with the front cover picture of the *Lord of the Isles* a few years earlier, around 1910 a note of informality is creeping into the still-sober holiday attire, with 'the bunnet' beginning to replace bowlers and boaters, but does the somewhat spectral presence of the warship create a subdued mood in these holiday crowds? The trio of sailors who can be seen among the crowd in the foreground on the right are presumably crew members. These were years that witnessed an 'arms race', with much anxious mention of the 'two power standard', that is, the government's perceived need to have a war fleet to match those of any two combined enemy nations, and as the *Vital Spark*'s engineer observed, 'If ye havenae Dreadnoughts ye micht as weel hae dredgers.' Such preoccupations, though, don't seem to have affected passenger numbers.

The cars and steamer of the Loch Eck Tour are seen here at Inveraray. By the 1930s the car tour was ousting the more time-consuming horse and carriage excursions. Before that era the Loch Eck tour could involve a three-in-hand carriage from Dunoon to Cowal's largest sheet of fresh water, a seven-mile sail, and another coach ride to Strachur, or on through to Inveraray via St Catherines and Cairndow, a 40-mile trip. Loch Eck more than rivals many longer, better-known lochs in sheer drama and grandeur, and the road, effectively the only route into Cowal, hugs the loch for its entire length. Even on today's swift bus ride, this is a thoroughly enjoyable journey. Better still is the walk along its facing roadless shore, where old tales and traditions from distant ages can become disturbingly credible. The steamer berthed here is unidentified.

The Church of All Saints at Inveraray stands in the shadow of the town's 126-foot bell tower, a corner of which can be seen at the far left. The church was built in 1886 by the 8th Duke of Argyll, himself Presbyterian, for his Episcopalian wife. Far-sighted in a pre-ecumenical era, he intended it for interdenominational use and today Roman Catholic mass is also said within. Inside is the font 'of blue Kilcatrine stone' belonging to 'Parson Kilmalieu', the real-life cleric mentioned in Neil Munro's *John Splendid* and appropriately surnamed MacVicar, himself arguably a pioneer of ecumenism since, up-ending the font, he hollowed out a second basin on the underside for christening Protestants at the Reformation. He is reported in *John Splendid* as declaring, 'There's such a throng about Heaven's gate that it's only a mercy to open two.' While some recent building has intruded behind the church, a tranquil atmosphere survives, but it is very much in the shadow of the newer, taller structure, completed in 1932 as a memorial to the Campbell dead of the Great War. Many view this as a real intrusion, a jarring note on the Inveraray skyline, but viewed from the south, towards dusk, its mellowed red granite merging with the greenery on Duniquaich, it looks magnificently, defiantly Scottish.

Inveraray Castle, home of the Dukes of Argyll, was built between *c*.1744 and *c*.1773. The '45 Rising crushed, the 3rd Duke turned his energies to erecting a dwelling worthy of a nobleman, replacing the crumbling, barely habitable chief's keep by the River Aray, although that was not wholly demolished until 1810. His clearance of the 'castleton' was not entirely welcomed, one ousted householder cementing his household goods into the new park wall in protest. Architects Roger Morris and later Robert Mylne, with substantial help from the better remembered Adam family, were employed under three dukes on a 50-year redevelopment project. After a fire in 1877, the uppermost storey was added, but note the absence of the distinctive 'witch's hat roofs' in this 1890s photograph. Fire again damaged the castle in 1975 and Marion Campbell describes how the banner-staffs were already aflame when the Argyll and Sutherland Highlanders' colours were rescued, while the duke ripped down a sagging ceiling with a pike last borne at Culloden.

While few criticise the splendour of Inveraray Castle's interior, not all warm to the sombre 'lobster blue' Kilcatrine stone (a variety of slate) from across the loch. The castle blends well, though, with its wooded surroundings of some 2 million trees in a 30-mile circumference, some planted by royalty, others by such notables as Gladstone and Tennyson. Despite this vast acreage of wood, water and hill, there are no formal gardens, but the grounds yield other attractions in the way of ancient standing stones, Celtic crosses, an old limekiln and a 10-foot brass cannon, designed by Cellini, salvaged from a wrecked Armada vessel off Tobermory. The flag flown is the Galley of Lorne, allowing the sour or cynical a jibe about how the *Grumach*, the only chief to be Marquis, twice escaped on such a vessel, leaving his clansmen to face the combined forces of Montrose and Left Handed Coll. The interior houses impressive displays of paintings, statuary, weaponry, armour, tapestries, porcelain, and Rob Roy's sporran and the hilt of his dirk, discovered near the site of his home in Glen Shira.

MALTLAND BY INVERJRAY E6.

There has been some speculation as to how and from where this view was obtained. The foreground foliage looks like treetops rather than hedgerow, and around 1910 neither flight nor photography was so advanced as to be able to secure low-level aerial shots. The complex of Maltland in the castle grounds was part of Mylne's rebuilding project, his design lending an 'urbane symmetry and scale to a group of farm buildings', a view with which a 'disgusted' Wordsworth disagreed, declaring 'the stables and outhouses or farm houses behind the castle … broad, out-spreading, fantastic and unintelligible buildings'. The name Maltland tells us that barley, if not actually grown here, was processed in a brew-house and there were probably facilities for producing a 'stilling' sited here, along with the 'magnificent drying barns … stables, smithy, wright's shops and dairies'. The original 'riding house', burned down 1817, was later replaced by the Jubilee Hall, copied from Mylne's original design. That too is gone, some of its timbers incorporated into the decor of the George Hotel.

Inveraray Pipe Band.

The Inveraray Pipe Band is assembled before the castle doorway, but the absence of tenor drums and drum major's mace suggests that it may not be the full band. Is it, then, just a group of selected players gathered for some occasion or function, possibly staged indoors? Is the man with the bow tie the 'pipey' or someone attending in a non-musical capacity? These questions go unanswered and none of the players has been identified, but it is probable that within a decade, some of these would have played troops into action in Flanders. There cannot be many better venues for hearing and seeing pipers than Winterton Park within the grounds of Inveraray Castle where the annual Highland Games are held each July, in the presence of a Highland chief. Led by the Duke, the band marches from Church Square to the grounds.

In 1757 William Douglas contracted to put up this new 40 foot by 17 foot water mill, whose ruins are still clearly visible, although shrubs, ferns and ivy are now reclaiming the site at Miller's Linn. The boiler-suited figure to the left of the buildings is presumably the miller of the time, in the first decade of the twentieth century. Neil Munro described how, after rains, 'the Aray roared at the cataracts below Carlunan Mill'. His spelling differs from that on the Ordnance Survey map, Carloonan, and the writer of this postcard mentions 'Carloonan House', probably referring to the house seen here above the mill.

'As the trek cart keeps rollin along', some of us used to sing around the campfire, although, in summer 1911, these laddies of the 4th Argyll Troop seem grateful that it has stopped. Writing on the back of the picture on the left suggests they are in Glen Lean, so if they are headed for the Ardgennavan site, between Dunderave and Cairndow, there's a lot more trundling 'over hill, over dale' before them. A 1910 Para Handy tale dealing with 'spy scares' explains the alarm as due to Germany's eagerness to invade these isles 'afore the Boy Scouts gets any bigger'; the movement, begun in 1908, had clearly caught on in a big way. Ardgennavan, 'the height by the sands', was journey's end for the lads at their camp, probably so hungry that 'even the smoke from the fire smelled good enough to eat'.

'Beetling against the breakers, very cold, very arrogant upon its barren promontory', Dunderave Castle gave Neil Munro the setting and title for his *Doom Castle*, although barrenness is hardly a feature of the promontory – it is so leafy along the shores that it is difficult to catch a glimpse of this fastness on its own side of the loch. Like the Campbells after them, the *MacNachtans* were incomers, both clans living in amity in Glen Shira and Glen Fyne until an outbreak of plague urged MacNaughton to build a new keep. The name may mean 'fort on the promontory', or, just as probably, 'fort of the two oars', since as part of their tenure they were obliged to provide Argyll with a two-oared ferry should he wish to journey on these upper reaches of the loch. 'Enthusiastic raiders when opportunity arose', they became alienated from the Campbells over their adherence to the Stuart cause and the clan was 'out' under Viscount Dundee at Killiecrankie. The last MacNaughton chief, seemingly victim of a deception, fled with his Campbell bride to Ireland, where the heads of the clan have since been known as the Baronets of Dunderave. Campbell of Ardkinglas took possession of the castle.

A broken clan after the 1715 Rising, the MacNaughton clansmen remained a 'troublesome Jacobite enclave' and again 'put the pole to the banner' under Charles Edward in 1745, some returning from Ireland to muster for 'the cause'. One, Honest John, was part of that garrison left holding Carlisle, where he was hanged. There appears to be more dereliction than drama in this picture of Dunderave Castle, taken before 1911 while Sir Robert Lorimer was carrying out the renovation of the five-storey sixteenth-century stronghold. Better known examples of his work are the Chapel of the Thistle in St Giles' Cathedral and Edinburgh Castle's National War Memorial, but he came up with a couple of masterpieces, Dunderave being one, here on Loch Fyneside.

Tell the bus driver you want Cairn-*dow* and he'll politely correct, 'Oh, ye mean Cairn-*doo*' ('black' or 'dark cairn'). The Cairndow Hotel, now called the Stagecoach Inn, is always worth a visit. In common with Crarae, Cairndow was one of those places long troubled by the 1752 re-jigging of the calendar, the inhabitants no longer certain whether the old or new date was the proper occasion on which to greet the New Year. Cautiously, they celebrated the 'Old New Year after a first rehearsal with the statutory one'. This old building must make a splendid rehearsal premises. Keats, despite poor health, walked the thirteen miles from Arrochar to here, celebrating his arrival by scratching his name, with a diamond, on a window pane. The landlord, unimpressed by such flamboyance, replaced the pane. William and Dorothy Wordsworth, accompanied by Coleridge, caused some hilarity with something resembling a 'jaunting car'. Mirth was probably an unfamiliar response to a pair more given to complaining comparisons with their beloved Lake District.

ARDKINGLAS MANSION LOCHFYNE FE

'One of the most graceful houses of Argyll', magnificently combining the finest features of Scottish architecture, Ardkinglas is not yet a century old, however primitive the technology involved might appear. Built in 1907 by Sir Robert Lorimer, before his restoration of Dunderave (its neighbour diagonally across the loch), the house is of a stone so mellow that the building can be difficult to pick out from the opposite shore. The seaward-facing gallery shown here is at the rear of the house. Ardkinglas was a Campbell barony extending to Lochs Goil and Long, one family head being the Sheriff of Argyll who, in good faith, administered the belated oath of loyalty to Mac Ian of Glencoe in 1692. In 1905 the estate was bought by the Noble family, one of whom became Secretary of State for Scotland. A more recently deceased member of the family did much to promote the local produce, known to have boarded a New York flight with a single sample of salmon and returning with a worthwhile order.

Right: Commanding a fine view towards Strone Point and Inveraray beyond, Tighcladich, or *Tigh Cladich*, 'the house by the shore', a few miles from St Catherines, seems exposed, even bleak, on its open brae, back in the 1920s. For all its closeness to the road, Tighcladich is now so well hidden from it by very tall trees that these buildings are traceable only by total reliance on the Ordnance Survey map.

Below: The view towards the bridge on the opposite shore, the castle just beyond, the 'sparkling quartzite' look of Inveraray itself, made the pier at St Catherines a pleasant spot to await the ferry (seen approaching) before 1965. The small pier is directly seawards of the local hotel, a common arrangement, the ferryman of old being readily granted permission to brew and sell ales and other fare, this 'perk' helping to make up for enforced idle hours with no passengers, or the free passage accorded to priests, pilgrims and the infirm. Kilcatrine – *kil* in place-names denoting cell, church or chapel – may itself have been a place of pilgrimage, although quite which saint of that name was venerated remains uncertain. The inn was at one time a coaching inn, popular with cattle drovers, later with walkers and anglers. From this same spot was shipped the stone that built the new Inveraray Castle.

TICHLADICH, ST. CATHERINES

St Catherines

Closed for some three decades, now an enviable private dwelling, the school at St Catherines has an idyllic setting by the loch's edge, possibly a distraction in itself to the scholar and a temptation to those with a taste for truancy, both strongly discouraged in the near-legendary 'wee schools of Argyll'. This is a relatively large one, many being one-roomed, the class containing pupils aged from five to twelve years, rigidly ruled by a 'dominie', or more usually, a lady teacher, generally recalled with admiration and affection. Here weans 'learned their letters' and what we now style the work ethic. In a sense, four Rs were taught – including religious instruction. Older, more accomplished pupils were often set to teach the younger or slower. Youngsters, often shoeless, regularly, and eagerly, walked lengthy distances to attend.

The historian George Eyre-Todd, finding 'no temptation of any kind to keep the pedestrian in Inveraray', decided on a night-crossing to the hotel at St Catherines (seen here in the 1920s), explaining how, 'with a gale blowing up Loch Fyne, there is a pleasant spice of adventure in the two-mile crossing'. He told how the ferrymen 'about the fire in their black-raftered waterside tavern are nothing loathe, and soon the stout little lugger is laying down her brown sail before the roaring wind and sheets of spray, as she heads for the inn light on the farther shore'. A 'scramble over black rocks slippery with seaweed' in the darkness only heightened his appetite for the 'excellent Highland cheer' with a 'parlour sofa by way of a bed'. It's an enviable little escapade of the pre-car era, after which (a probably less informal) hospitality was extended to 'travellers on wheels', rather than venturesome nocturnal voyagers.

At the end of St Catherines pier (sloping to cope with the states of the tide, and more of a slipway) can be seen, in this view of around 1913, the gangway used for boarding the ferry. On the verge above the beach are the poles on which nets were hung to dry or when undergoing repairs. The timber structure at the tide's edge was possibly used for penning beasts whose owners sought 'refreshment' in the hotel while watching for the ferry. A short way down the lochside is what some claim to be the smallest post office in Britain. This was politely corrected by the friendly lady behind the counter, with the information that there is a 'smaller one on one of the islands'. Its size may restrict any range of wares, but a peckish walker coming across it isn't likely to worry about lack of selection.

Known as Strachur Pier, this is properly speaking Creggans Pier, as Strachur once had its own pier a mile or so along the loch, though never one where steamers could berth. Here, around 1922, is the *Queen Alexandra*, 'consort' to the *King Edward*, the first commercial turbine-powered passenger steamer, built at Denny's Dumbarton yard in 1901. 'Lean and very silent in motion', the *King Edward* was so popular that the *Queen Alexandra* immediately followed. Ill-suited to short pier-to-pier runs, the two were put on the long trips to Campbeltown and Inveraray and back to Greenock where, refuelled, they would turn around to do evening cruises (Arran, Ailsa Craig, the Kyles). At 3 shillings for some four hours of sailing, these were a delight and terrific value. Around this period the pier was noticed to be in poor repair and a dozen years later was closed. There is no evidence today of the piles, and the pierhead (seen just beyond the tree) is now a grassed seating area where stands the re-sited MacPhun's Cairn. Hitting hard times, MacPhun was sentenced to hang for sheep-stealing. His wife, nursing a newborn child, went to collect the body, detected signs of life and revived her spouse with a mixture of mother's milk and whisky. Already executed according to law, he could not be re-tried and happily he lived to recover his fortunes.

The gable on the left of the upper view of the Clachan, Strachur, belongs to the smithy, and if Mr Montgomery, the smith of the day (around 1909), looked across the road, he might have cast an eye towards the ground his business would come to occupy. Robert Anderson's wee shop is today the agreeable Clachan Inn, surely nowadays the licensed premises with the shortest distance between bus stop and entrance (the alighting passenger couldn't get damp on the wettest of nights). The smithy is still here, having reopened for a time.

In the lower view of the Clachan, Strachur, a war has intervened, a conflict that introduced many to motorised transport, and Mr Montgomery has expanded, diversifying from shoeing horses to servicing and selling their replacements. The shop, minus its signboard, is still trading, possibly benefiting from the new business across the way, while the adjoining property has acquired a front garden. The more modern shop, with the sloping roof, has sprung up behind the old inn, while there is new tree growth around the churchyard. A length of the wall, though, between houses and inn has been removed, possibly because unsafe or perhaps some road widening was now called for to accommodate Montgomery's customers. Certainly his business was no nine-day wonder, since the garage was demolished only very recently, its site at present being redeveloped.

What would James Bond do on retirement? Well, a decade or so back, you might have been both shaken and stirred to find him owner of Creggans Inn at Strachur, famous for its restaurant and pub. Brigadier Sir Charles Fitzroy MacLean was held to be the 'original' for Ian Fleming's 007. Cameron Highlanders, wartime SAS, 'Churchill's man' with Tito's partisans in Yugoslavia, diplomat, MP, traveller, explorer, author and historian, he makes the mere Commander Bond look something of an under-achiever. From 1957 he made this premises highly respected for its cuisine, but there is still the small, informal MacPhun's Bar to the left of the building, where walkers can meet 'sib souls'. The inn, as the stacked herring boxes indicate, faces the old steamer pier, seen here shortly before the First World War. While there are no motor vehicles to be seen and there is still evidence of a coaching trade, the bicycle has by this time evolved to look fairly modern.

Landlord of the inn as he was, Fitzroy MacLean did not live 'above the shop', but bought the eighteenth-century Strachur Park when he purchased Creggans. The house, where the ailing Chopin was once a guest, had been built by a General Campbell on lands once belonging to the MacArthurs, who regarded even the long-settled MacLachlans (of Norse origins) as raw newcomers and boasted of how 'The Devil and the hills came into the world at the same time but when came Clan Arthur?' Well enough disposed to 'Clan Diarmid' to style themselves MacArthur-Campbells or even Campbells of Strachur, they had for a time their clan seat here at Strachur. The rather fine mansion can be glimpsed from the road towards St Catherines, its wing additions now re-built to harmonise with the original building.

Not far from Strachur Park, the tiny but conveniently sheltered bay at Strachur was a small port or harbour serving the settlements on this side of the loch. Here wherries, gabbarts, herring 'skiffs' and puffers moored, catches were unloaded, and sheep and cattle put ashore – Strachur being once known for its own cattle fairs – whence the beasts could be herded towards the inland trysts or southwards. Only a line of slimy stumps now remains to mark the site of the pier, from which this view was taken. Just behind where the photographer must have stood stands another testament to the sense and sensitivity of road-makers in this part of Argyll. Cutting down a 'sacred' rowan tree was to invite calamity, and two, so entwined as to become 'one tree with two trunks', that the authorities elsewhere might have felled, were carefully dug up and successfully transplanted to a spot near the old pierhead. The houses, in this view from the first years of the last century, are here still, not greatly altered, but caringly maintained. The narrow doorway makes the two-storey building perilously close to the tide's edge ill suited to serve as a boathouse, but it may have stored nets, lobster pots and boat repairing gear. Note how some of the rowing boats feature fixed wooden pegs to house the oars, rather than the more familiar movable rowlocks.

Shamrock-like, Strachur consists of three separate, tenuously linked, settlements, creating a population similar to that of the more compact Inveraray across the loch. Most live here in 'the Clachan', tucked away from both waterside and main road by 'the stream of the dark falls'. The church dates only from 1789 but the circular graveyard proves the existence of much earlier places of worship and medieval gravestones are set into the walls of this building. There is also a watch-house from the grisly era of the body-snatchers. Opposite is the sizeable inn, no longer a licensed premises today, and, striking a jarringly modern note, is what looks like an industrial unit, but was seemingly built as a shop although it served later as a timber yard and workshop.

The Newton was new in the late decades of the eighteenth century, made necessary by the infamous Clearances, perhaps less harsh in this corner of Argyll than elsewhere in the Highlands. Despite the clan's involvement in Prince Charlie's campaign, the MacLachlans regained their long-held lands, but all chiefs, stripped of former powers and authority, were mere landowners, forced to make these lands pay. The solution appeared to be in the introduced 'sheep with the big teeth' or 'the sheep that ate the men'. Hills and glens had to be cleared of the clanfolk settled there, but the MacLachlan chief offered alternative land by the coast to develop a fishery. There was always a demand for catches, but it was an unpredictable trade and there were periods when even the fishers were forced to gather shellfish. Few could have a truly viable amount of land and depopulation continued. In this view the fishery would seem still to be a going concern, judging by the array of posts beyond the distant house. On these nets were draped for drying, 'barking' and mending. This is still a delightful place, worthy of a less prosaic (or older) name, although forestry has somewhat altered its appearance.

Castle Lachlan, begun around 1790, was home to more than one chief designated 'Lachlan MacLachlan of Strathlachlan, Castle Lachlan, Strathlachlan, Strachur', so we can assume that their mail was generally delivered to the correct address. They had been in possession through long centuries for, while they claimed kinship with the Royal House of Ulster, *Lochlan* was the Gaels' word for the Vikings' homeland, hinting that they may have held these lands since the days of the 'dragon ships' with Odin's raven on their sails. This replaced the spectacular old clan seat by the loch's edge, pounded by Royal Navy cannon after being embarrassingly garrisoned in the chief's absence by Campbell militia. His absence was due to his calling out his clansmen, from both sides of Loch Fyne, to 'rise and follow Charlie' in the summer of 1745 and as he marched them off, his mount made an ominous anti-sunwise turn. Serving as ADC to the Prince, MacLachlan fell in the final battle at Culloden, where MacLachlans and MacLeans had fought as one combined regiment. The horse is said to have returned, swimming across Loch Fyne and passing its remaining days in the shadow of the old castle.

CASTLE LACHLAN LOCHFYNE FE

If reckless adherence to the Stuart cause was a MacLachlan virtue, so seemingly was forgiveness, for despite the injury done to his ancestral seat by the Royal Navy, one chief served that force diligently enough to become an Admiral. The German High Seas Fleet surrendered to him in 1918, which accounts for the presence in Strathlachlan's church of the 'Jack' flown on the *Royal Oak* at Jutland and the White Ensign flown when he accepted the surrender at Scapa. The church dates from 1792 but the ruin of the much older Kilmorie (Church of Mary) from medieval times can be seen in its ancient graveyard. The forge, the white building on the left, is gone.